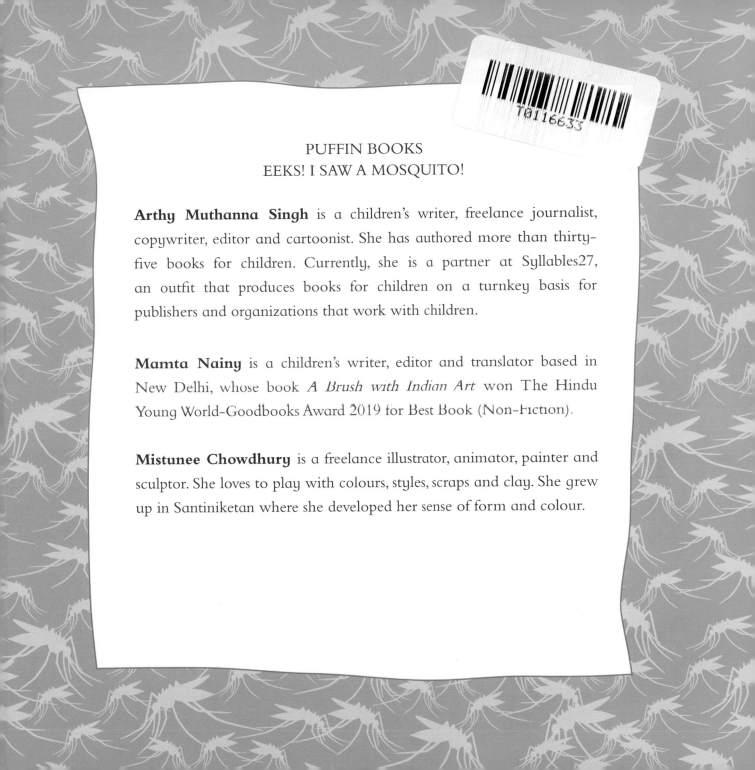

PUFFIN BOOKS
EEKS! I SAW A MOSQUITO!

**Arthy Muthanna Singh** is a children's writer, freelance journalist, copywriter, editor and cartoonist. She has authored more than thirty-five books for children. Currently, she is a partner at Syllables27, an outfit that produces books for children on a turnkey basis for publishers and organizations that work with children.

**Mamta Nainy** is a children's writer, editor and translator based in New Delhi, whose book *A Brush with Indian Art* won The Hindu Young World–Goodbooks Award 2019 for Best Book (Non-Fiction).

**Mistunee Chowdhury** is a freelance illustrator, animator, painter and sculptor. She loves to play with colours, styles, scraps and clay. She grew up in Santiniketan where she developed her sense of form and colour.

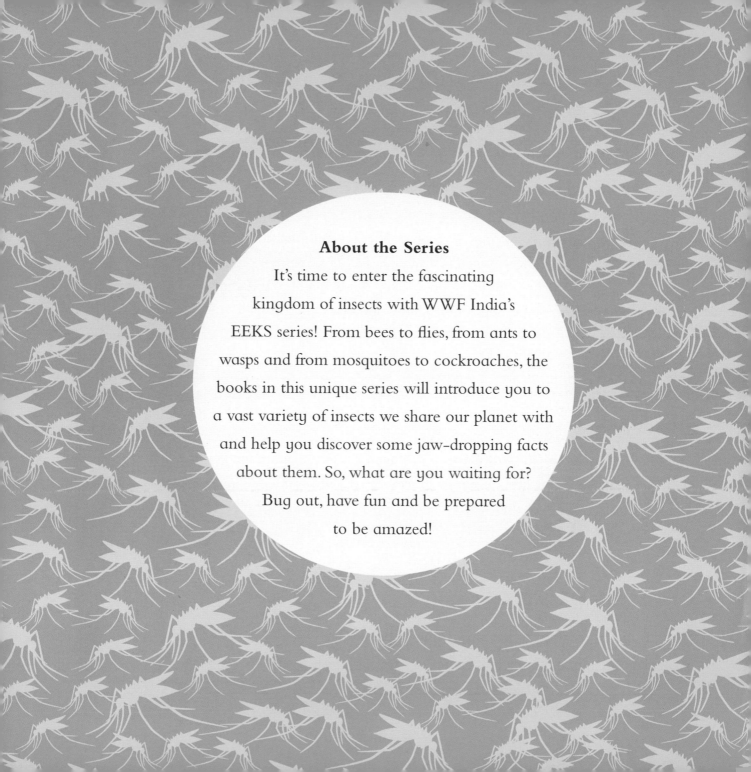

**About the Series**

It's time to enter the fascinating
kingdom of insects with WWF India's
EEKS series! From bees to flies, from ants to
wasps and from mosquitoes to cockroaches, the
books in this unique series will introduce you to
a vast variety of insects we share our planet with
and help you discover some jaw-dropping facts
about them. So, what are you waiting for?
Bug out, have fun and be prepared
to be amazed!

..........................................

is about to
enter the
amazing world of
**insects!**

PUFFIN BOOKS

USA | Canada | UK | Ireland | Australia
New Zealand | India | South Africa | China

Puffin Books is part of the Penguin Random House group of companies
whose addresses can be found at global.penguinrandomhouse.com

Published by Penguin Random House India Pvt. Ltd
No: 04-010 to 04-012, 4th Floor, Capital Tower -1,
M G Road, Gurugram -122002, Haryana, India

First published in Puffin Books by Penguin Random House India 2021

Text and illustrations copyright © World Wide Fund for Nature-India 2021

ISBN 9780143451020

Layout and design by Aniruddha Mukherjee
Typeset in Bembo Infant by Syllables27, New Delhi
Printed at Aarvee Promotions, India

www.penguin.co.in

# EEEEEEKKKS!

## I SAW A
## MOSQUITO!

Arthy Muthanna Singh and Mamta Nainy

Illustrations by Mistunee Chowdhury

PUFFIN BOOKS

An imprint of Penguin Random House

# EEEEEEKKKS!

Mosquitoes are insects,
I don't want to hear.
Circling round my head,
And buzzing by my ear!

I think they're always hungry,
And looking for some skin,
To quietly descend on,
And bite right in!

What are the four words you think of when you see a mosquito?

1. ................................
2. ................................
3. ................................
4. ................................

BOO!
Did you know that the fear of mosquitoes is known as anopheliphobia (ano-phel-i-pho-bia)?

# MAYA'S BUZZING WIN

It was the last ball of the last over of the game. The match was between C Block Champs and G Block Go-getters in the Colony Cricket League. But everyone knew that the C Block Champs would win because the best batsman of their team, Neil, was going to bat. The score was 53 and he needed just one more run to take his team to victory.

Maya, the youngest member of G Block Go-getters, got ready to bowl the last ball. She was the only one in her team who had not given up yet. She took a short run and swung the ball towards Neil.

Neil moved forward to hit the ball. Just then he heard something buzzing near his ear. He felt something bite him on his neck. He raised his hand to smack it when suddenly . . . CRACK! The ball brushed past his bat and went towards the wicketkeeper.

'How's that?' appealed the surprised wicketkeeper, holding the ball up in his glove.

The umpire raised a finger.

Maya was the first one in her team to start dancing with joy!

## TINY LITTLE CREATURES

Has this ever happened to you? You're in the park, playing with your friends, when suddenly you hear something buzzing in your ear. And then you feel a familiar mild sting on your arm. You slap it hard but miss it. And immediately you see a red mark appearing on your arm. Scratch, scratch! It's itchy too! You know exactly who fed on you—a mosquito, of course.

Mosquitoes can be irritating—we all know this—but do you know that they can be fascinating too? Come, let's examine these tiny creatures and learn more about them!

# MEET THE MOSQUITO

A mosquito (mus-kee-toe) is a tiny flying insect. In fact, the word 'mosquito' means 'a little fly' in Spanish and Portuguese. There are around 3000 kinds of mosquitoes found in the world, and only a few are harmful to humans.

You will always know when mosquitoes are close because of their buzzing! They're usually between a centimetre or two in length and weigh around 2.5 mg. Even though they are so very tiny, they are not scared of anything or anyone. Female mosquitoes are particularly fearless, since they're the ones who actually bite. They primarily feed on plant nectar for the energy they require, but they also need protein to produce eggs. The source of the protein is from a tiny meal of blood, which they get from various animals including humans. So, when you're sleeping and suddenly hear a high-pitched 'zzzzzzzzzzzzz' sound, you know it's a tiny lady mosquito trying to get its next meal from you!

# LIVING IT UP

Would you believe us if we told you that mosquitoes have been living on Earth for millions of years? Yes, it's true! Scientists have found an ancient fossil of a mosquito that was trapped in a shale rock. And guess what? It had a blood meal inside its tiny belly that was 46 million years old—a solid evidence of the existence of bloodsucking mosquitoes even in ancient times!

But millions of years ago, mosquitoes were much larger than what they are today! As the years passed, they changed and adapted to the environment and can be found everywhere, though there are fewer of them in marine, Arctic and Antarctic regions. You can even find mosquitoes in deserts, but they're only active when it rains. There's only one country where mosquitoes aren't found—Iceland!

A FOSSILIZED MOSQUITO TRAPPED IN AMBER

# LOOK CLOSELY!

Every mosquito's body has three main parts. The head holds the parts that sense light, sound, heat and smell. The middle part called thorax has wings and legs attached to it. The abdomen is where the digestion or breakdown of food happens.

Have you ever wondered why mosquitoes buzz? Mosquitoes can sense carbon dioxide even from 100 ft away. So when we exhale it through our mouth and nose, mosquitoes are attracted towards our head and they circle around it to slyly snack on us. They move their tiny wings around 600–1000 times per second and that's what creates the buzzing sound. Just like a fan!

Long antennae that detect smells. A female's antennae are slender and have only a few strands of hair.

A soft body with a hard covering

Large eyes that have a huge number of individual lenses that point in all directions and move independently

A mouthpart called proboscis that looks like an upside-down funnel with a strawlike end to suck blood

Anyone who's tried to swat a mosquito knows how quickly the insects can evade a blow. Mosquitoes have compound eyes, which provide a wide field of view, and are largely responsible for such lightning-fast actions.Researchers have now developed compound lenses inspired by the mosquito eye that could someday find applications in autonomous vehicles, robots or medical devices.

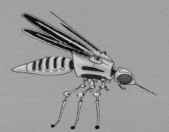

Meet a ROBOTIC MOSQUITO!

## EXOSKELETON

Mosquitoes, like all insects, are cold-blooded. They don't have a skeleton the way we do, i.e., inside the body. They have an exoskeleton, a hard exterior shell that protects what's inside. When a mosquito grows, it sheds its exoskeleton and grows a new one!

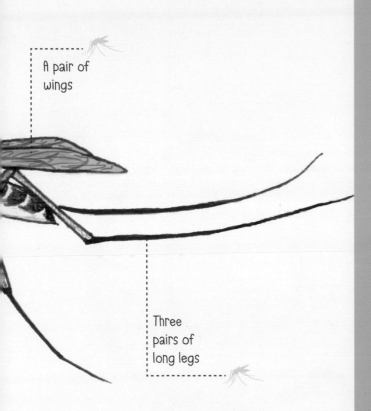

A pair of wings

Three pairs of long legs

PARTS OF A MOSQUITO

# IT'S A MOSQUITO'S LIFE!

Y ou know, don't you, that each insect goes through a set of stages, or changes, called the life cycle? Mosquitoes are no different; they go through four stages of development and their full life cycle takes about a month. Mosquitoes can live as long as five or six months, but few survive that long. Most live for less than three weeks!

Female mosquitoes find the people she can bite (you too!) by sensing human odour and detecting the warmth of your body. After drinking blood, adult females lay 40 to 400 tiny white eggs in water that does not flow or very slow-moving water (you may have seen these floating on water but thought it was just dirt). Within a week, the eggs hatch into larvae that shed their skin four times as they grow and are then called pupae.

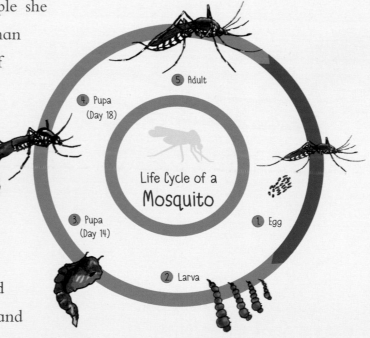

5 Adult

4 Pupa
(Day 18)

Life Cycle of a
**Mosquito**

3 Pupa
(Day 14)

1 Egg

2 Larva

Pupae do not eat. An adult comes out from a pupa when the skin splits after a few days and it is ready to fly into its life of buzzing!

## WINTER VACATIONS

Think about how we all prepare ourselves for cold winter months. We wear coats, gloves and boots to stay warm. We eat soup and drink yummy hot chocolate. And there's nothing like spending the day sleeping under a warm, cosy quilt, is there? Some female mosquitoes also spend the winters sleeping. They go into what is called hibernation during winters. The adult females of some species find holes where they wait for warmer weather and sleep for up to six months!

1. Mosquitoes who bite at night start looking for places to sleep as soon as daylight comes.

2. Some mosquitoes bite in the day as well as the night, and so they sleep at different times.

3. Mosquitoes sleep like you and I do, but unfortunately, they don't like to sleep at the same time we do! Most mosquitoes are busy at night or evening and early morning; they rest or sleep during the day.

4. Mosquitoes don't sleep lying down. They rest in the same position as when they land on you to have a meal!

# SO MANY MOSQUITOES

There are about 3000 species of these little creatures worldwide, buzzing from the Arctic Circle to the equator, from the lush tropical Amazonian forests to the icy tundra. You will be surprised to know that there are some parts of the Amazon rainforests where human beings cannot live because of mosquitoes carrying malaria and yellow fever! But many species of mosquitoes are not harmful to humans, because they do not carry diseases.

Mosquitoes like sheltered places, such as brush or thick weeds, caves or rock shelters, holes in the ground, hollow logs or holes in trees. When they live close to people, they use whatever we have built, hiding in basements, small gaps under roads, in cupboards or any dark place where they think they won't be disturbed.

# MOSQUITO MADNESS

Out of the many species of mosquitoes found worldwide, more than 400 can be found in India, and they are all carriers of diseases—so beware! After all, one of them might be resting in some dark corner of your house right now or if you're reading this on a warm summer evening, raising a faint buzz—do you hear it?—in your ear! These are the groups of mosquitoes that we are going to be reading about now.

## AEDES

One of the most dangerous types of mosquitoes, this mosquito is about 4 to 7 mm in length and is black in colour with light and dark bands. It is most active during daytime and can fly small distances. It also feeds on human blood and causes deadly diseases like dengue fever, Zika fever, yellow fever and chikungunya. Its eggs take about 6-8 days to turn into an adult mosquito. It breeds in containers, especially man-made containers with clean water, such as old discarded tyres, plastic bottles, etc., which collect rainwater.

4-7 mm (*Aedes aegypti*)

15

# ANOPHELES

The name Anopheles comes from a Greek word meaning 'useless'. The Anopheles mosquito is about 5 to 6 mm in length and is dark brown in colour. These mosquitoes usually live near swamps, ponds, pools and places where wild plants grow. They usually bite at night and then rest during the day. The female Anopheles is the only type of mosquito that causes malaria. Their eggs take about 6-10 days to become an adult.

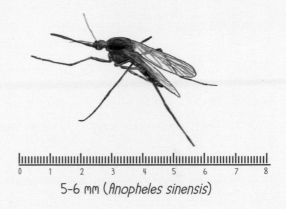

5-6 mm (*Anopheles sinensis*)

# CULEX

Dull and dusty brown in colour with faint white bands across their bodies, the Culex mosquito is much more dangerous to animals and birds than to humans. These mosquitoes carry encephalitis, filariasis and the West Nile virus. They are most active during the night and rest indoors before and after their meal. They mainly breed in polluted, stagnant water and drains, and their eggs take about 6-10 days to become adults.

3-5 mm (*Culex pipiens*)

# WHAT'S ON THE MENU?

Some people think that mosquitoes feed only on blood, but that's not true at all. Both male and female mosquitoes suck delicious nectar from flowers. Only the female mosquitoes suck blood. But why, did we hear you ask? That's because blood has special nutrients that help in producing eggs. Her special mouthparts can pierce through the skin. Now you know one way to tell male mosquitoes from females!

## SCRITCHY-SCRATCHY STUFF

Have you ever wondered why you get an itchy bump when a mosquito bites you? Here is why: When a female mosquito sits on you and bites, she often sucks four times her weight of your blood. Wait, there's more! While sucking blood, the female mosquito injects you with her saliva (spit). This saliva causes a mild allergic reaction and an itchy red bump.

Just like some of us like pizzas more than burgers or smoothies more than ice creams, mosquitoes too have very specific tastes. Different mosquito species like the blood of different animals.

Some mosquitoes prefer the blood of snakes and frogs, some like the blood of birds while some others feed on cows, horses and people. But there are some mosquitoes that bite whatever they find, such as crows, jays, robins, sparrows, ducks, geese and herons—exactly like some of us who will eat just about anything!

# GOOD NEWS!

Mosquitoes are yummy to eat and they are easy to catch—well, not for us, but many birds, frogs and species of fish like to eat them! The mosquitofish could go extinct if there were no mosquitoes, as their main food is mosquitoes. Hundreds of species of fish would have to change their food habits to live. Not easy! In waterbodies, while other insects drown, the mosquito larvae feed on waste products, making nutrients such as nitrogen for the plants. Without mosquitoes, there could be a problem with the growth of water plants.

19

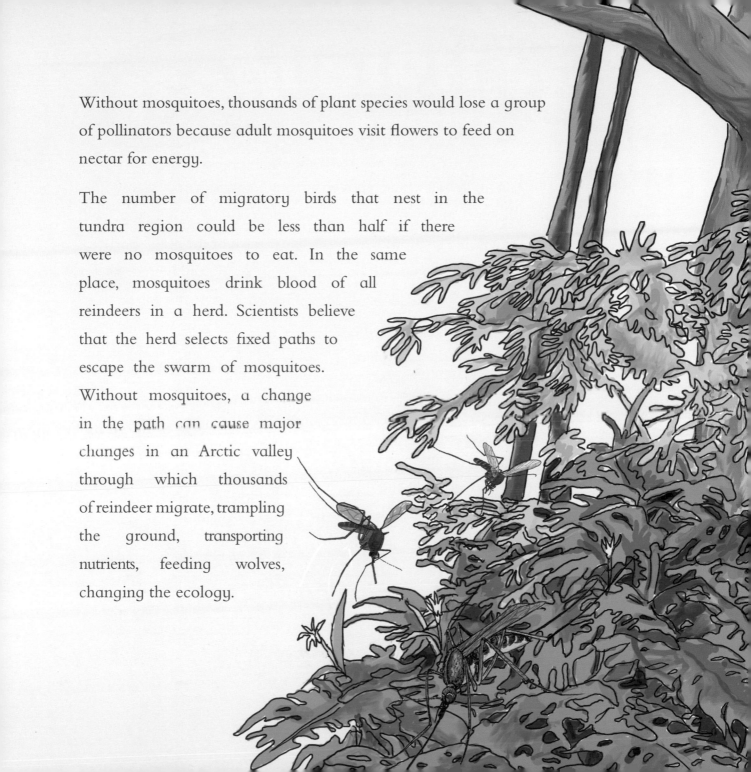

Without mosquitoes, thousands of plant species would lose a group of pollinators because adult mosquitoes visit flowers to feed on nectar for energy.

The number of migratory birds that nest in the tundra region could be less than half if there were no mosquitoes to eat. In the same place, mosquitoes drink blood of all reindeers in a herd. Scientists believe that the herd selects fixed paths to escape the swarm of mosquitoes. Without mosquitoes, a change in the path can cause major changes in an Arctic valley through which thousands of reindeer migrate, trampling the ground, transporting nutrients, feeding wolves, changing the ecology.

# MIGHTY MOSQUITOES

Think about it: What would happen to the environment if one day—poof!—all the mosquitoes simply disappeared? If you just said 'How wonderful!', then think again, because each of the 3000 species of mosquitoes are very important in nature. For example, male mosquitoes eat nectar and help pollinate some crops and flowers. Mosquitoes are eaten by all kinds of animals such as fish, turtles, dragonflies, frogs, birds, snakes and bats, making them an important food source for the ecosystem.

Also, the tiny mosquito protected the top predator for centuries. The Terai region was free from humans for centuries because it was a swampy area full of mosquitoes. This allowed tigers to live happily there. So that makes mosquitoes useful! However, when DDT—a synthetic organic compound used as insecticide—started being used, all this changed. People moved in and destroyed the tiger's habitat.

## BUT . . .

But, as we know, some species of mosquitoes carry the world's worst diseases and each year, hundreds of thousands of people die from malaria, dengue fever and chikungunya after being bitten by a disease-carrying mosquito. So it's best to stay away from these tiny but mighty insects!

## GOING, GOING, GONE!

Do you know that the world's most invasive mosquito species has been almost completely wiped out from two islands in China? Scientists and researchers in China have managed to reduce the population of the female Asian Tiger mosquito—which was the main source of bites and disease transmission on these islands—by up to 94 per cent.

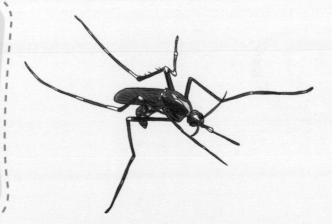

# WATCH OUT!

So while our environment does need these tiny creatures, there's no reason why we shouldn't protect ourselves from them! Here's how we can do that:

1. The best thing you could do to keep mosquitoes away is to prevent them from breeding in your locality. Mosquitoes lay their eggs in water. So you need to empty or cover anything that holds water.

2. Mosquitoes can be prevented from entering your houses by making sure that windows and doors have screens with no gaps.

3. Try and wear long-sleeved shirts, long trousers and socks if you spend time outdoors during peak mosquito-biting hours. Wearing half-sleeved shirts,

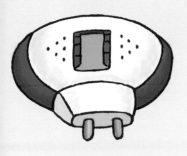

T-shirts and shorts during July to September, which is usually the season for dengue and malaria, is not a good idea.

4. Apply insect repellents, especially while playing outside. The use of mosquito repellent sprays, creams, coils and mats are also great to keep the mosquitoes at bay.

5. Avoid popular mosquito hang-outs. Go where the mosquitoes are not!

6. Keeping your surroundings and your neighbourhood clean will also go a long way in preventing the spread of diseases. Ask everyone to help.

## DID YOU KNOW?

Mosquito repellents don't repel—they actually hide your scent so that the mosquito cannot figure out that it's you!

## WHAT MOSQUITOES LIKE AND WHAT THEY DON'T

| LIKE | DON'T LIKE |
|---|---|
| Warm, cosy and moist environments | Clean spaces |
| Stagnant, slow-moving water. Any pool of water, even a little in the saucer of a plant pot or caught inside an old tyre, is a good place for them to stay. | Dry water containers such as water tanks, tube wells, etc. |
| Marshes and swamps | Predators who eat them such as bats and birds |
| Humans to feast on, especially sweaty ones! | Mosquito repellents, coils and mats |
| Sweaty feet | Plants that repel them such as citronella, rosemary, basil, etc. |
| Dirty socks | Humans who kill them |

## TEENY TINY THINGS

Now you know to keep your houses and neighbourhoods clean so that you can be safe from the tiny creatures. And in case you do see some mosquitoes around, just hope and pray they are males and not females!

### LAUGH OUT LOUD!

What's the difference between a fly and a mosquito?

A fly can fly but a mosquito cannot mosquito!

### ELEPHANT MOSQUITO

Toxorhynchites, also called elephant mosquito, breed in tree holes and its larvae are predatory on the larvae of harmful mosquitoes. When they become adults, they visit flowers and aid in pollination.

S o mosquitoes don't really deserve an EEKS, do they? Now, write four things that you think are amazing about mosquitoes.

1. .............................................................................................

2. .............................................................................................

3. .............................................................................................

4. .............................................................................................

## ASIAN TIGER MOSQUITO

The Asian tiger mosquito, found in tropical regions of South East Asia, has black and white stripes on its body like the tigers.

## SOME FUN WORDS TO KNOW ABOUT MOSQUITOES

1. **Tumbler:** The pupa is also called a tumbler.

2. **Wriggler:** Larva is also called this because they swim or wriggle through the water.

3. **Raft:** The eggs form layers called rafts that float on the water.

4. **Wheal:** The small itchy swelling on the skin caused by a mosquito bite.

5. **Stylets:** Mouthparts that a mosquito uses for cutting.

Did you know?

1. A group of mosquitoes is called a scourge.

2. The world's deadliest creature isn't a shark or a tiger, it's a mosquito! The Aedes aegypti mosquito, which spreads the Zika fever and thirty other diseases, is the world's deadliest creature.

3. You get bitten more by mosquitoes if you wear dark-coloured clothes because dark colours absorb heat.

4. The female mosquito is the only insect that can spit and suck at the same time.

5. The best time to avoid mosquitoes is in the afternoon, when temperatures are hottest and the insects rest in cooler spots.

## Activity 1

Apart from mosquitoes, which other insect makes you say EEKS?
Draw and colour it.

# Activity 2

Think of a new species of mosquito and name it. Now draw it in the box below. Try it; it'll be fun!

## Be a critter spotter!

Our backyards are filled with small fascinating creatures. Go outside and explore the world of insects. Make notes of all the insects that you spot—their sizes, shapes and colours. To help with the exploration, carry a magnifying glass. Make sure you take time to observe. Take photos of the bugs you see or draw their pictures. Write down which bugs you see and where you saw them. From watching a centipede dig in the soil to seeing a bee interact with a flower, there is no limit to the number of things you can discover. But do remember that you're like a giant for a teeny bug—they might get scared of you! Watch them, but don't touch them or pick them up.

## More reading on insects

https://kids.nationalgeographic.com/animals/invertebrates/insects/

https://www.si.edu/spotlight/buginfo/incredbugs

https://theconversation.com/birds-bees-and-bugs-your-garden-is-an-ecosystem-and-it-needs-looking-after-65226

https://www.coolkidfacts.com/insect-facts/

https://kids.britannica.com/

# Insect Identification Sheet

Date: ....................                      Time: ......................

| Draw the insect | Habitat of the insect |
|---|---|
|  | Describe where they are generally found in the world |

1.    How many legs does the insect have?

2.    Does the insect have wings?

3.    Can you see its eyes?

4.    What colour is it?

5.    How many body parts does it have?

6.    Does it fly, hop or crawl?

Name of the insect: .................................................................

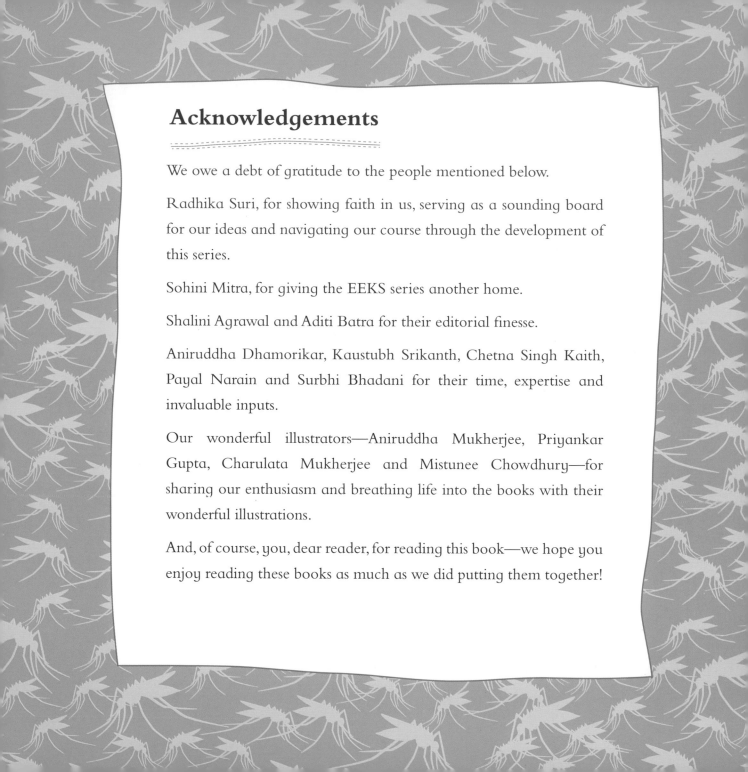

# Acknowledgements

We owe a debt of gratitude to the people mentioned below.

Radhika Suri, for showing faith in us, serving as a sounding board for our ideas and navigating our course through the development of this series.

Sohini Mitra, for giving the EEKS series another home.

Shalini Agrawal and Aditi Batra for their editorial finesse.

Aniruddha Dhamorikar, Kaustubh Srikanth, Chetna Singh Kaith, Payal Narain and Surbhi Bhadani for their time, expertise and invaluable inputs.

Our wonderful illustrators—Aniruddha Mukherjee, Priyankar Gupta, Charulata Mukherjee and Mistunee Chowdhury—for sharing our enthusiasm and breathing life into the books with their wonderful illustrations.

And, of course, you, dear reader, for reading this book—we hope you enjoy reading these books as much as we did putting them together!

# About WWF India

Marking fifty years of conservation in the country, WWF India works towards finding science-based and sustainable solutions to address challenges at the interface between development and conservation. Today, with over seventy offices across twenty states, WWF India's work spans thematic areas including the conservation of key wildlife species and their habitats; management of rivers, wetlands and their ecosystems; climate change adaptation; driving sustainable solutions for business and agriculture; empowering local communities; combatting illegal wildlife trade; and inspiring children and youth to take positive action for the environment through education and awareness programmes. WWF India is part of the WWF International Network, which has offices in more than 100 countries across the globe.

Environment Education has been a core part of WWF India since its inception in 1969. It continuously works to inform and empower the children, youth and citizens of India to act and create impact for a sustainable planet. Its initiatives reach out to diverse audiences and aim to create a generation of critical thinkers, problem-solvers and environmentally aware individuals.

# Read More in the Series

 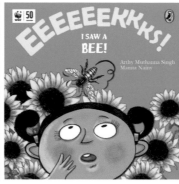 

Ants are small but that's not all! Enter the jaw-dropping world of ants and explore some interesting facts about one of the most hard-working critters of the insect kingdom!

What's the buzz about bees? What do they do all day? Why are they important? Find out everything about bees in this buzzing book and discover the big ways in which these little insects contribute to our environment.

Whether cockroaches fill you with dread or wide-eyed wonder, there's no denying the fact that they are some of the most amazing creatures of the insect universe. So, dash right into their wonderful world, find out everything about them and be prepared to be super surprised!